the life of a flower

Melanie Goldring

BookLeaf Publishing

India | USA | UK

Presentation by *BookLeaf Publishing*

Web: www.bookleafpub.com

E-mail: info@bookleafpub.com

ISBN: 9789358318845

First edition 2023

this is dedicated to all of those who have had their flowers withered or taken away too soon

the song of your body

missed beat
your body
sings a new tune
broken melody
strings snapped
fingers sore
i call
chicken wings today she says
bring me flowers tomorrow she says
suck your lolly
goodbye i say
and go to sleep

observations

oxygen mask abandoned
too weak to have the help
breathe alone
in your tummy
you don't even flinch
at the needle
but if someone
moves your pineapple
chaos erupts in your mind
you wish to walk
but your legs
have blown with the petals

25th October

head hangs low to feed
on the cheese and custard creams
you ask for your beef drink
half goes down the sink
television on high
i slip out
no goodbye

the life of a flower

your hands
itch to move it
closer
as though that
one inch
would make
a difference
but your fingers
can't grasp
what has happened
in your head
you will be here
after all the lilacs
but nan i wish
you were a zinnia

care

5

the sun will get up tomorrow
but you won't
unless they make you
pull you
encourage you
you say they hurt you
i say they help you
okay she says
calm down
i'll open the curtains
you can have your cinema
of the policeman in the house opposite
that calms you down
now tell me again
how did you meet Grandad

damage

boiled bubbling blood
but who to blame
not you
you fell
they repaired the damage
and sent you away
the woman that touched
her toes daily
and asked if i was
courting lately

concerns

so stubborn
fair enough you're ninety-seven
one hospital trip
seven weeks on the drip
only thing that bothered you
who's gonna make me a brew?
what is the point?
every joint causes pain
but grandma don't worry
it will all be okay
but how do i know?
a hammer bangs me awake
scared today is the day
but the carers mark the book
no concerns today

daily routine

i paint your face in the wind
watch it blow around the street
before it disappears entirely
you left me a space in the kitchen
to wash your clothes daily
but you can't wear these now
i wash them anyway and
fold them into a pattern that
reminds you of your first house

mood change

fire your aims
at my ears
i can hear them
you ask why i cry nan
then you cry and
i cry more
then my dad cries
and my heart breaks
into twenty uneven pieces
and i water them and
watch the stem grow
and you whisper
where's my kfc

jenga

words queue in your throat
like a jenga tower
but it keeps climbing
until you let it out
all at once and we don't understand
you whisper for a pizza
that you know you're not allowed
now you're in trouble and
you fold your arms and frown at the telly
but i won't take your attitude nan
i'll leave it on the doormat
wrap it up and tuck it in beside you
and watch as it slides back into you

walking stick

11

she asks for her stick
not for walking, but to hit
it hits like a brick

petals

bones become more visible
delicate to touch
and if we do it hurts
and if we don't it hurts
shrinking like a violet
yet as loud as a rose
with petals falling
onto our hands
we catch them and
blend them into tea
but you won't drink it

the dreaming room

the dreaming room
of chaos mixed with
a dash of tranquility
for your mind's sake
and your mind only
i'll clean the carpet
around you
wipe your hands too
while you sleep for seconds
then look at the clock
that you can't see and say
well i must be dreaming

potatoes

they say potatoes have a long life
if you store them correctly
you must've been a potato in another life
because you're as ripe as any
not like the berries that will only last a day
or the oranges that change colour
you fill yourself with pineapple
and stay ripe like a strawberry

thoughts

the painter slashes the canvas
the writer rips the page
the performer breaks their leg
i paint a plane and wish you there
how did you age so quickly?
i feel your cries in my bones
keep on waddling said the penguin

friend of the stars

meg ryan meg ryan
is that meg ryan?
who we all say
is that meg ryan?
nan, we say,
tom hanks i've got his number she says
no wonder your phone bill is so high
if you're calling america nan

i've never played bingo

i was never good at sleeping
whichever way i lay it's painful
and you said the carers aren't helpful
even though they closed the curtains
and poured the tea
they never played bingo

or anything close to bingo
bring your knees up to sleep
be careful, don't knock your tea
that will cause more pain
like opened curtains
now that's not helpful!

can i come and help
you play this game of bingo
they're in the way those curtains
and i don't want to sleep
either way it causes us pain
i give you one cup of tea

please you want some tea
can i help
your leg too is painful
the dabber for bingo

sorry i fell asleep
twenty minutes ago i lost the curtains

i can't see the curtains
you've spilt your tea
in my sleep
i don't need any help
let's get to bingo
and forget our pain

it's disappeared this pain
maybe it's in the curtains
i don't know the way to bingo
or if i have sugar in tea
nobody can help
i must now sleep

you need no help, only sleep
there is no pain please drink the tea
close the curtains for your everlasting bingo

i salute you goodbye

please take a small breath
i say this once - i care
about all of the flowers
on their earth filled beds
waiting to complete their journey
wave them goodbye nan

take a bow nan
for you can breathe
on this part of the journey
and take pride in your care
for others stuck in bed
please pick your flower

to match Grandad's flower
and choose it slowly nan
your rose-filled bed
isn't ready for its first breath
all we want is to care
for this final journey

onwards to the safe place the journey
will hold in both hands your flowers
that signal the care
all these people had for you nan

take a deep breath
and reserve your place on the bed

you will find comfort on that bed
and on this journey
as you take small breaths
and hold all the flowers
you've gathered, nan
please take care

i will continue to care
for all the people in bed
just like you were nan
on different journeys
holding different flowers
taking longer breaths

Nan, i ask you take care
a deep breath into bed
on this last journey held by flowers

moving on

now is the time to reflect
one year on,
we left the flowers
in a neat little parcel
and i believe
that was your shadow

behind the tree, your shadow
dances in the wind and reflects
what i fully believe,
as time moves on
the paper loosens on the parcel
and those wilted flowers

tell me how to grow a new flower
how to follow in your shadow
to protect every parcel,
fairy lights reflect
your voice i can only hear on
old videos, but i believe

in what you told me to believe
where i was told to lay the flowers,
as you moved on
i saw you everywhere, your shadow

showed me where to go, i reflect
on wrapping your last parcel,

placed it with the other parcels
shipped it straight to the sky, believe
in the light that reflects
those pretty flowers
you once picked, the shine of a shadow
moves you on

through the clouds you go on,
higher, in time for your parcel,
there is no shadow
up here, you believe
in the flowers
from your back garden, reflect

in time i hope to reflect on all the shadows
on my journey to believe
collecting your flowers to make my own parcel

blink and you'll miss it

blink and you'll miss
how fast they have to fly
one day they're rocking in their chair
the next they're a cloud shape in the sky
and though you knew this day would come
it may be better that they're back where they
belong

and if where they belong
is anywhere near you, then they'll be missing
you too, you come
and visit their garden, you watch them fly
with other clouds in the sky
but where they should be is their armchair

and since they left us, you can't sit in that
armchair
it's like it doesn't belong
to you, if you could just send it up to the sky
it might go some way to solving the problem of
missing
you, if i could fly
i'd come

straight to you, i'd come

through stormy sunshine just to bring you your
chair
but i can't fly
and they tell me i belong
here on the ground, so i'll just be missing
you from down here, sometimes i wave to the
sky

i don't know if you notice, but i do wave to the
sky
and i dream of you coming
back down and saying i missed
you too, and i'll point to your chair
and you'll finally be back where you belong
but you'll have to fly

away again, and i don't think i could take
another flight
to the sky
if you can't be where you belong
then i hope you'll come
and visit, you chair
will always be empty missing

i belong here for now, but one day when i fly
up to that sky, i'll tell you all you've missed out
on
and you'll say 'come, sit in my chair'

garden

i like to visit your garden
where time stands still
and i can dream of you
holding pretty pink flowers
shadows dance across graves
but it's calm here, i could sit

and read a book to you, i'll take a seat
in your dear little garden
amongst the other graves
time sits still
here like a child holding flowers
as they make their way to you

they lay them at your bed, you
would smile and sit
at the edge, holding your precious flowers
there's something calming about this garden
i feel relaxed in its presence, like you're still
here somewhere, behind a grave

waiting to greet me, but my face was grave
this was serious, you weren't you
i couldn't reach you, but i still
felt close to you, if i could just sit

there in your garden
i'll bring you flowers

and wait everyday, i'll tidy the flowers
as i walk past the graves
until i reach your garden
resting place, i feel your
presence as i sit
somewhere in your company, still

i have to leave sometimes, i'm still
alive, i dream of you floating with flowers
as i take my seat
the other graves
begin to talk to me to you
about your dream garden

it's hard to sit still
when i visit your garden, my flowers
could pick any grave, but they chose yours

www.ingramcontent.com/pod-product-compliance
Lightning Source LLC
LaVergne TN
LVHW051249200726
843510LV00011B/1760